— POCKET —
MASSAGE
— FOR —
STRESS RELIEF

CLARE MAXWELL-HUDSON

DORLING KINDERSLEY

LONDON • NEW YORK • STUTTGART • MOSCOW

A DORLING KINDERSLEY BOOK

Massage Photography Sandra Lousada
Editor Nell Graville
Designer Helen Diplock
DTP Designer Karen Ruane
Senior Art Editor Tracey Clarke
Managing Editor Susannah Marriott
Managing Art Editor Toni Kay
Production Controller Patricia Harrington

Important Notice

Refer to the safety precautions on page 22 before using any essential oil. Do not try self-treatment during pregnancy, or for serious or long-term problems, without consulting a doctor. Seek medical advice if symptoms persist. Neither the author nor the publisher can be held responsible for any damage, injury or otherwise resulting from massage or the use of any essential oil.

First published in Great Britain in 1996 by
Dorling Kindersley Limited,
9 Henrietta Street, London, WC2E 8PS

Copyright © 1996 Dorling Kindersley Limited, London
Text copyright © 1996 Clare Maxwell-Hudson
Massage photography © 1988, 1994, 1996 Sandra Lousada

All rights reserved. No part of this publication may be reproduced, stored in a retrieval system, or transmitted in any form or by any means, electronic, mechanical, photocopying, recording or otherwise, without the prior written permission of the copyright owner.

A CIP catalogue record for this book is available
from the British Library

ISBN 0 7513 0270 8

Reproduced by Colourscan, Singapore
Printed and bound in Italy by LEGO

CONTENTS

INTRODUCTION

THE ART OF MASSAGE reaches beyond the recorded history of the oldest civilizations, yet unlike other traditional therapies, its value in promoting health is verified by scientists today.

STRESS RELIEF

We all need some stress to add zest to life, but when it becomes too much and we fail to cope with it, stress can be detrimental to health. Research in Ohio, U.S.A., for example, found that the immune system of students was far weaker during exam periods than after a relaxing holiday. Ailments such as headaches, backache, insomnia and digestive disorders are all more likely to occur when our resistance to infection is lowered through stress. To deal with stress effectively, we need to be in control, and be aware of our levels of anxiety and exhaustion. Massage helps us to do this by teaching us what it feels like to be really relaxed.

MASSAGE FOR WELL-BEING

Massage soothes the body and mind, and is thought to instigate the flow of endorphins – opiate-like substances – through the body. In doing so, it improves our well-being and evidence shows that feeling good and having a positive outlook boosts health. A 1995 study at the Royal Marsden Hospital, London, analysed the response of cancer patients to a weekly massage. After eight weeks, patients not only felt more optimistic, but showed great improvement in levels of pain and mobility.

THE POWER OF SCENT

Essential oils enhance the benefits of massage. At Middlesex Hospital, London, in 1994, post-cardiac patients were offered either conversation, a rest, a foot massage with unscented oil or one with fragrant neroli oil. Both massage groups had lower anxiety rates than the control groups, yet those receiving neroli oil felt more positive.

SHIATSU SELF-HELP

According to the oriental therapy of shiatsu, good health is maintained by the energy of life, or chi, that flows through the body along channels known as meridians. Each meridian affects a major organ and its related functions. When the body experiences stress or illness, the chi is disrupted. Pressing firmly on the skin at precise points along the meridians restores its flow and promotes well-being. Alongside the massage techniques and advice on essential oils in the book, I offer shiatsu self-help sequences.

This book came into being in response to requests from students at my school, health professionals and members of the public for a pocket-sized massage guide. I hope it will help you to manage your stress. Happy massaging!

Clare Maxwell-Hudson.

STRESS-RELIEVING ESSENTIAL OILS

*This is my personal selection of essential oils,
chosen for their relaxing and restorative qualities,
and their ability to soothe or refresh.*

Chamaemelum nobile / Matricaria recutita

CHAMOMILE

CHAMOMILE IS A GENTLE OIL with a powerful herbaceous aroma. It is my first choice for treating conditions that need calming and soothing, whether stress, irritated skin or muscular aches.

Chamomile oil is soothing and anti-inflammatory.

THERAPEUTIC PROPERTIES

Roman chamomile (*C. nobile*) is often used for emotional upsets, while blue German chamomile (*M. recutita*) has a superior anti-inflammatory action. Both are sedative and antispasmodic.

C. nobile

Emotional stress: Calming. Allays anxiety and insomnia.

Physical stress: Use to soothe muscular pains and headaches.

Skin conditions: Add to a bath blend to treat allergies.

Digestive disorders: Use in stomach massage to ease flatulence.

Cautions: See page 22.

The flowers of both varieties of chamomile yield the oil

M. recutita

> ### KEY USES
> ❖
> Insomnia: page 58
> Jet lag: page 53

Citrus aurantium
ORANGE

THE BITTER, OR SEVILLE, orange tree yields three essential oils: orange, neroli and petitgrain. All are used to calm the nerves and combat stress. The fresh, familiar aroma of orange oil is gently uplifting.

Use orange oil to calm and refresh.

THERAPEUTIC PROPERTIES

Native to Asia, Seville oranges were reputedly introduced to Europe by the crusaders around AD1200. They were used to treat the nerves and indigestion in 18th-century European herbal medicine.

Emotional stress: Calming and uplifting. A general tonic.

Skin conditions: Mildly astringent. Use in facial massage to revitalize the skin.

Digestive disorders: Use in massage to ease indigestion.

Cautions: Avoid sun/sunbeds for 6 hours. See page 22.

KEY USES
❖
Stomach aches: page 78
Backache: page 72

The rind of the fruit produces orange oil

Citrus aurantium
NEROLI

WITH AN EXQUISITELY sweet, intense aroma, neroli is prized for its gentle sedative nature and is a classic remedy for stress. Petitgrain, from the leaf of the bitter orange tree, is lighter and less expensive.

Use sweet neroli oil as an antidote to stress.

THERAPEUTIC PROPERTIES

Neroli oil is valued for its tranquillizing quality. It helps to combat depression, relax the mind and soothe the nervous system.

Emotional stress: Use in massage to counter insomnia and pre-menstrual tension.

Skin conditions: Add to a massage blend to treat sensitive skin and acne.

Digestive disorders: Use in stomach massage to ease irritable bowel syndrome.

Cautions: Avoid sun/sunbeds for 6 hours. See page 22.

KEY USES
❖
Relaxing bath: page 89
Vaporizer: page 91

The blossom of the bitter orange tree yields neroli oil

Lavandula angustifolia / L. officinalis

LAVENDER

POPULAR AND VERSATILE, lavender oil has a piercing, floral scent and has long been recommended as a folk remedy for insomnia. Low dilutions are now used to help hospital patients sleep well.

Lavender oil is calming and sedative.

THERAPEUTIC PROPERTIES

The oil is used primarily as an antiseptic and for its sedative effect on the nervous system.

Emotional stress: With its ability to calm and sedate, lavender can help counter insomnia or jet lag.

Physical stress: Analgesic and antispasmodic. Use in massage blends to relieve headaches and muscular pains; in inhalations to alleviate colds and influenza.

Skin conditions: Antiseptic. Apply diluted oil to spots, acne, eczema and insect bites.

Cautions: See page 22.

> ### KEY USES
> ❖
> Insomnia: page 58
> Headaches: page 66

The flowering tops are distilled to extract the oil

L angustifolia

Mentha x piperita

PEPPERMINT

REFRESHING AND COOLING, peppermint has a fresh, minty, balsamic aroma and is a highly effective mental stimulant. It is traditionally used as a digestive remedy to alleviate stomach aches.

Use peppermint oil to clear the head.

THERAPEUTIC PROPERTIES

Research has shown that peppermint improves alertness and stimulates the brain without altering the heart rate.

Emotional stress: To revive the spirits, inhale a couple of drops of oil placed on cotton wool.

Physical stress: Decongestant, cooling. Add to a massage blend to combat headaches and colds, and to refresh tired feet.

Digestive disorders: Analgesic, antispasmodic. Use in stomach massage to relieve indigestion.

Cautions: Avoid in pregnancy. Use a 1% dilution. See page 22.

> ### KEY USES
> ❖
> Stomach aches: page 78
> Hangovers: page 64

Peppermint leaves are partially dried to produce the essential oil

Origanum majorana
MARJORAM

REVERED SINCE ANCIENT TIMES as a symbol of contentment and well-being, marjoram is a pungent herb from the mint family with a sweet, warm aroma. I use it to quieten the mind and ease taut muscles.

Marjoram oil is warming and soothing.

THERAPEUTIC PROPERTIES

Dioscorides, the Greek herbalist, recommended marjoram for soothing the nerves. Japanese research has confirmed its sedative, antifungal and antibacterial actions.

Emotional stress: To restore jangled nerves and induce sleep, use in a massage or bath blend.

Physical stress: Rubefacient, antispasmodic and relaxant. Use in massage for stiff muscles, and in inhalations for congestion.

Cautions: Avoid in pregnancy. Use a 1% dilution. See page 22.

> ### KEY USES
> ❖
> *Sports aches: page 80*
> *Restorative bath: page 89*

The flowers and leaves yield the essential oil

Pelargonium 'Graveolens'

GERANIUM

GERANIUM OIL has a sweet, floral aroma that resembles rose. It is a useful skin-care oil and is said to have a calming effect on both emotional and physical conditions. I often use it in facial massage.

Use fragrant geranium oil to reduce tension.

THERAPEUTIC PROPERTIES

Geranium was traditionally used to staunch bleeding, and treat skin and digestive disorders. Its antibacterial actions have been confirmed and it is also an insect repellant.

Emotional stress: Antidepressant, relaxant. Use in a massage or bath blend to regulate mood swings related to pre-menstrual tension.

Skin conditions: Suits all skin types. Use in facial massage to treat sensitive skin and acne.

Cautions: Use a 1% dilution. See page 22.

The whole plant is distilled to make the oil

KEY USES
❖

Jet lag: page 53
Mental fatigue: page 92

Rosa centifolia / R. damascena

ROSE

SINCE ANTIQUITY, *the healing properties of rose oil have been celebrated. Roses are traditionally associated with Venus, the Roman goddess of love and beauty, and the oil continues to be used to uplift the spirits.*

Use rose oil as an antidote to depression.

THERAPEUTIC PROPERTIES

Avicenna, a 10th-century philosopher and physician, said rose oil "increases the might of the brain and quickes the mind". It is expensive, but only a little oil is needed for effect.

Emotional stress: Antidepressant. Add to a bath blend for pre-menstrual tension. Bulgarian research found that it also aids alertness.

Skin conditions: Antibacterial, antiseptic. Suits all skin types. Use in facial massage for dry, sensitive skin and eczema.

Cautions: See page 22.

Rose petals are the source of the essential oil

R. centifolia

KEY USES
❖
Lethargy: page 63
Inhalation: page 44

Rosmarinus officinalis

ROSEMARY

ROSEMARY OIL has a fresh herbaceous aroma and is noted for its revitalizing, uplifting effect on both the body and mind. According to 17th-century herbalist Culpeper, it helps to "quicken the senses".

Rosemary oil is refreshing and stimulating.

THERAPEUTIC PROPERTIES

Rosemary is renowned for its invigorating qualities and has been shown to stimulate the central nervous system. It was traditionally used as a fumigant to combat infection.

Emotional stress: Add to a bath blend to allay fatigue.

Physical stress: Rubefacient. Use in massage for muscular pain, congestion and headaches.

Skin conditions: Use in massage to refresh the skin and scalp.

Cautions: Avoid in pregnancy, high blood pressure and epilepsy. See page 22.

> ### KEY USES
> ❖
> *Aching legs: page 34*
> *Headaches: page 66*

The flowers yield the oil

Salvia sclarea

CLARY SAGE

IN ROMAN TIMES, clary sage was thought of as a cure-all. The oil has a warm, nutty aroma and is a powerful relaxant. I use it on clients who are convalescing after hospital to promote a sense of well-being.

Use clary sage for its antidepressant qualities.

THERAPEUTIC PROPERTIES
In high doses, clary sage can leave one feeling almost stupefied and euphoric.

Emotional stress: Potent sedative. Add to a bath blend to treat depression, nervous fatigue and insomnia.

Physical stress: Antispasmodic, warming, analgesic. Use in abdomen massage for period pains and muscular aches.

Skin conditions: Anti-inflammatory and soothing. Add to a facial massage blend.

Cautions: Avoid in pregnancy; avoid alcohol. See page 22.

> ### KEY USES
> ❖
> Stomach aches: page 78
> Relaxing bath: page 89

The leaves and flowers are the source of the oil

Santalum album

SANDALWOOD

CALMING TO THE BODY and mind, and noted for its warm, oriental aroma, sandalwood is used in incense throughout the East. It is one of my favourite oils for luxurious, pampering massages.

Sandalwood oil is soothing and calming.

THERAPEUTIC PROPERTIES

Sandalwood is traditionally used to calm and cool the body, and reduce inflammation and infection. Long-lasting, it is often used as a perfume fixative.

The heart wood of the tree trunk produces the oil

Emotional stress: Sedative. Enhances a sense of well-being. Can help to alleviate anxiety and depression.

Physical stress: Use in inhalations for chest tightness, sore throats and bronchitis.

Skin conditions: Soothing, anti-inflammatory. Use to treat acne, eczema and dry skin.

Cautions: See page 22.

KEY USES

❖

Relaxing bath: page 89
Colds & coughs: page 92

OTHER ESSENTIAL OILS

ESSENTIAL OIL	THERAPEUTIC PROPERTIES	KEY USES	CAUTIONS (See page 22)
Boswellia carterii / B. thurifera **Frankincense**	*Anti-inflammatory, antiseptic, calming, deepens breathing*	Back massage, uplifting vaporizer	*See safety measures, page 22*
Cananga odorata **Ylang Ylang**	*Sedative, euphoric, used to treat anxiety and depression*	After-work massage, restorative bath	*May cause headaches and nausea*
Citrus limon **Lemon**	*Refreshing, antiseptic, astringent, a tonic*	Inhalation for drivers or VDU users	*Use a 1% dilution; avoid sunlight for 6 hours after use*
Cymbopogon citratus **Lemon-grass**	*Antiseptic, analgesic, digestive tonic*	Refreshing room spray, insect repellant	*May irritate the skin; use a 1% dilution*
Eucalyptus globulus **Eucalyptus**	*Decongestant, antiseptic*	Compress for leg cramps, inhalation for colds	*Use a 1% dilution; avoid with homeopathic remedies*
Jasminum officinale / J. grandiflorum **Jasmine**	*Uplifting, antidepressant, used to treat lethargy*	Inhalation for VDU users, bath for lethargy	*Avoid in pregnancy and on babies*
Juniperus communis **Juniper**	*Antiviral, diuretic, antiseptic, local stimulant, refreshing*	Invigorating bath, uplifting vaporizer	*Avoid in pregnancy and with kidney disease*
Melaleuca alternifolia **Tea Tree**	*Antiviral, antibacterial, antifungal*	Inhalation for colds, first aid for cuts	*For sensitive skin use a 1% dilution*

CARRIER OILS & BLENDING

To avoid skin irritation, essential oils must be diluted in carrier oils before being used in massage. Carrier oils are effective moisturizers, helping to keep the skin smooth and supple, and they also contain vitamins, proteins and minerals.

CHOOSING CARRIER OILS

VEGETABLE CARRIER OILS, such as sunflower, sweet almond, apricot kernel, soya and grapeseed oils, are commonly used to dilute essential oils. Since they are used in far greater quantities than essential oils, carrier oils have an important part to play in the massage treatment. Experiment with different oils until you find ones that suit you. Other carrier oils such as avocado, jojoba and wheatgerm can be mixed in to enrich a blend. Adding 10–20% of wheatgerm oil also helps to prevent rancidity and extend the shelf-life. If possible, choose cold-pressed carrier oils for their high quality.

Sunflower oil

Soya oil

Sweet almond oil

Grapeseed oil

Apricot kernel oil

BLENDING OILS

TO MAKE AN OIL BLEND, first decide the effect you wish to achieve. Then choose suitable essential oils from pages 8–19, making sure the aroma appeals to you or your partner. Mix a few drops with carrier oil, following the guidelines below for safe dilutions. You will need about 20 ml (4 tsp) of oil for a full body massage, 10 ml (2 tsp) for a face massage.

Choose a carrier oil (or blend of oils) and decant the amount you need into a dark bottle. Select up to three essential oils (see pages 8–19), calculate how much to use (see below), and add to the carrier oil. Close the bottle, shake gently and label it.

GUIDE TO BLENDING OILS

❖

Normal dilution of 2½%:
ml carrier oil ÷ 2 = maximum drops essential oil
(e.g. 20 ml carrier oil ÷ 2 = maximum 10 drops essential oil)

Low dilution of 1% for sensitive skin and for use during pregnancy:
ml carrier oil ÷ 4 = maximum drops essential oil
(e.g. 20 ml carrier oil ÷ 4 = maximum 5 drops essential oil)

Extremely low dilution for very sensitive skin, children and babies:
1 drop essential oil per 10 ml carrier oil, or sweet almond oil by itself

---

SAFETY & STORAGE

ESSENTIAL OILS ARE HIGHLY concentrated and can cause irritation to the skin if too strong a concentration is used. Follow the recommended dilutions on page 21 and read the guidelines below before using essential oils.

SAFETY MEASURES

❖ *Always dilute essential oils before applying to the skin.*

❖ *Before using a new essential oil, place a diluted drop on the inner wrist, apply a plaster and check after 12 hours. If there is irritation, do not use the oil.*

❖ *Never take essential oils internally.*

❖ *If you are pregnant or have a medical condition, consult both a qualified aromatherapist and a doctor before using essential oils.*

❖ *Citrus oils increase sensitivity to sunlight. Avoid sunbathing and sunbeds for 6 hours after use.*

STORAGE TIPS

❖ *To avoid spoilage, store oils in dark glass bottles in a cool, dark place, with lids secured. To prolong the life of an oil, store in the bottom of the refrigerator.*

❖ *Label bottles with the oils used, dilution and date.*

❖ *Keep out of children's reach.*

❖ *Keep oils away from flames.*

❖ *Do not store on polished surfaces.*

❖ *Most essential oils deteriorate. Ideally, use them within 1 year, and within 3 months if mixed with a carrier oil.*

MASSAGE FOR
WORK & TRAVEL

*Relax and re-energize yourself or a partner with
these simple step-by-step massage sequences, devised
to ease away mental fatigue and physical tension.*

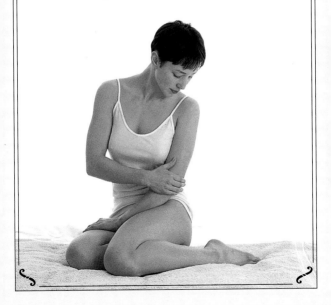

PREPARING TO MASSAGE

IN ORDER FOR A MASSAGE to disperse stress and replenish energy successfully, whether at home, in the office, or in an airport lounge, it is essential that both you and your partner feel as comfortable as possible. Try to find a quiet, warm space without harsh lighting where you can avoid interruption and concentrate on what you are doing.

BEFORE YOU BEGIN

If massaging a partner lying down, choose a firm surface such as a floor or large table padded with a futon, towels or blankets. Cover any exposed areas of your partner's body with towels to retain warmth. To avoid stiff knees, kneel on a cushion and try not to slouch.

For self-massage while sitting at a desk, or on a plane or train, keep your feet hip-width apart and your back straight.

Wear comfortable clothes for massage and remove jewellery. Relax, breathe deeply and enjoy the rhythm of the movements.

WARNINGS

❖ *If your partner is pregnant, see page 22.*

❖ *Never massage someone with any of the following conditions without a doctor's consent:*

• *inflammatory conditions, e.g. varicose veins or thrombosis*

• *acute back pain*

• *skin infection or bruising*

• *an infection, contagious disease or high temperature*

• *any serious medical complaint.*

USING MASSAGE OIL

MASSAGE OIL HELPS the hands glide over the skin and promotes smooth, even strokes. Make up an oil blend (see pages 20–21) and shake the bottle well before use. The amount of oil you need will depend on the area of the body you are covering and the dryness of the skin. Keep the open bottle within easy reach throughout the massage. If you need to apply more oil, keep one hand on the body while picking up the bottle.

APPLYING THE OIL

1 **Never pour oil** directly on to the skin. Pour a small amount into the palm of one hand and warm it between your palms.

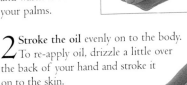

2 **Stroke the oil** evenly on to the body. To re-apply oil, drizzle a little over the back of your hand and stroke it on to the skin.

IN THE OFFICE

OVERWORK, DEADLINES and a constantly ringing telephone can all make office life stressful. Combat tension by learning to breathe correctly, and take ten minutes to try these self-massage steps while sitting at a desk.

MANAGING STRESS

I To induce calmness, practise slow, deep abdominal breathing. Place one hand on your chest and the other on your abdomen. Breathe in through your nose and allow the abdomen to expand. Then exhale through your nose, feeling the abdomen sink down. The hand on your chest should remain still.

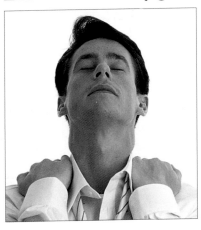

2 **Loosen your collar**, if necessary, and mould your hands over your shoulders. Exhale, letting your head drop back, and slowly draw your fingers down over your collar bones, stroking deep into the muscles to relieve tension. Repeat several times.

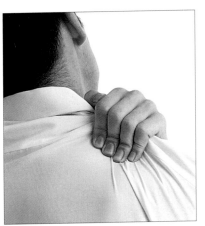

3 **Place your left hand** on your right shoulder by the neck and gently squeeze the flesh between your palm and fingers. Hold for several seconds, then release. Work along your shoulder and the top of your arm, wherever you can feel tautness. Stroke the whole area and repeat on the left shoulder.

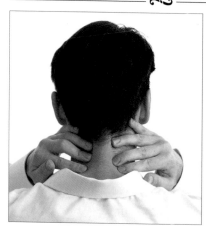

4 **Place the fingers of both hands** at the base of your skull on either side of the spine. Apply slow circular pressures, working down your neck and out across the back of the shoulders.

5 **Support your left elbow** with your right hand and firmly drum the fingers of your left hand across your right shoulder blade. Then stroke the whole area to soothe it. Repeat on your left shoulder.

6 **Place both hands** on the back of your head, interlacing your fingers. Drop your head forward, allowing the weight of your elbows to pull the head gently down. You should feel a stretch down the back of the neck.

7 **To banish any last vestiges of tension**, lift your right shoulder and slowly rotate it backward. Repeat with your left shoulder, then rotate both shoulders together, keeping your arms loose and relaxed.

MASSAGE FOR VDU USERS

SIMPLE SELF-MASSAGE STROKES help ease the eyestrain, stiff hands and repetitive strain injury that can follow hours spent working at a computer. Take a ten-minute break every hour and spend about five minutes on the face and two minutes on each hand. Inhaling a couple of drops of essential oil placed on cotton wool can also have a revitalizing effect.

RELAXING THE FACE

1 **First release any tautness** in your face. Cup your hands over your eyes and enjoy the relaxing darkness. Hold for several seconds.

2 **To alleviate headaches and eyestrain**, apply small circular pressures to your temples with the two middle fingers of both hands.

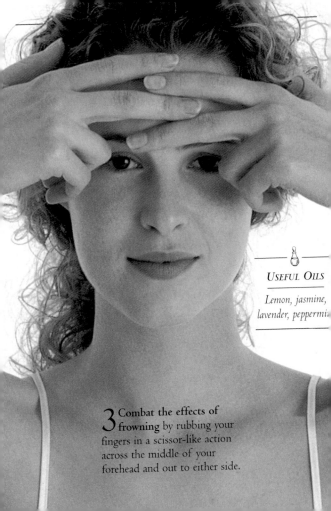

USEFUL OILS

Lemon, jasmine, lavender, peppermi

3 Combat the effects of frowning by rubbing your fingers in a scissor-like action across the middle of your forehead and out to either side.

SOOTHING THE HANDS & WRISTS

I **Relax each hand** by stroking across one palm with the heel of your other hand. Glide back, repeat, then work from the fingers to the wrist.

2 **Stretch the fingers** by holding each one at the base and pulling it firmly. Slide and twist your grip up the finger, then off at the tip.

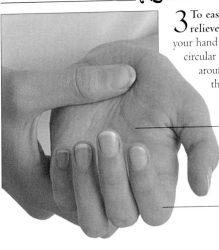

3 To ease the palm and relieve headaches, turn your hand over and make circular thumb pressures around the base of the thumb and all over the palm.

Apply pressure all over the palm using your thumb

Keep your fingers loose and relaxed

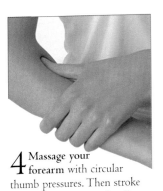

4 Massage your forearm with circular thumb pressures. Then stroke the whole area up to the elbow.

SELF-HELP TIPS

❖ *For the eyes, focus on each corner of a distant wall in turn.*

❖ *Stand up and stretch to the ceiling, then flop down to your toes. Repeat 5 times.*

❖ *Inhale essential oils. In a study, lemon caused 54% fewer errors in computer users, jasmine 33% and lavender 20% fewer.*

AFTER STRENUOUS WORK

MANY JOBS IMPOSE great physical strain upon the body: lifting heavy loads, performing repetitive tasks or standing for hours can cause aching muscles in the lower legs and feet. Self-massage of the legs eases stressed muscles and a foot massage renews vitality. Use diluted oils (see page 21) to increase the sense of relaxation.

EASING ACHING LEGS

I To relax tired leg muscles, place one hand on each side of your ankle and stroke smoothly up your calf to the knee. Repeat 5 times.

USEFUL OILS

Rosemary, marjoram, lavender, ylang ylang

Stroke both hands slowly and evenly up your calf

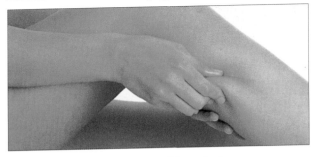

2 Stimulate your calf muscles by
kneading. Alternately squeeze and
release the muscles, first with one hand
and then with the other.

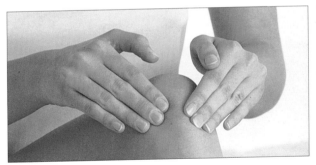

3 Soothe stiffness in the knee by
applying circular finger pressures
around the area. Then stroke behind your
knee. Repeat each step on the other leg.

REFRESHING FOOT MASSAGE

1 First relax the whole area. Rest your left foot on your right thigh and sandwich the foot between both hands. Then rhythmically stroke both hands together up from your toes to your ankle. Repeat several times.

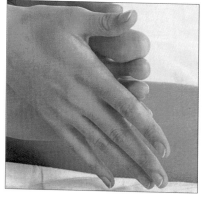

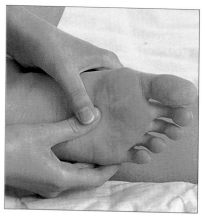

2 Make firm stimulating pressures with one thumb placed on top of the other down the centre of your sole. Repeat in a straight line down each side of the sole in turn.

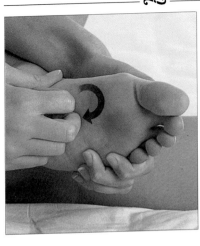

3 **To release any tense spots**, support your foot with one hand and make your other hand into a loose fist. Make small circular movements with your knuckles all over the sole.

4 **For an instantly invigorating effect**, hold your foot with one hand and lightly and briskly hack the sole with the side of your other hand. Finish by stroking all over the foot. Repeat the whole sequence on your right foot.

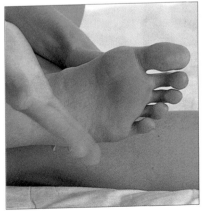

UNWINDING AFTER WORK

A SOOTHING NECK AND SHOULDER massage is the perfect way to release tense muscles and restore zest after a stressful day at work. Swap a massage with a friend. The receiver should sit astride a chair, using a cushion to lean on. The massage takes about ten minutes, and since it can be done through clothing, there is no need for oil.

Lean your weight *gently on to the shoulders*

SHEDDING STRESS

1 **To relax stiff, hunched shoulders**, stand behind your partner with your feet apart and rest your forearms on the fleshy area on top of each shoulder. Lean forward so that your body weight eases your partner's shoulders down.

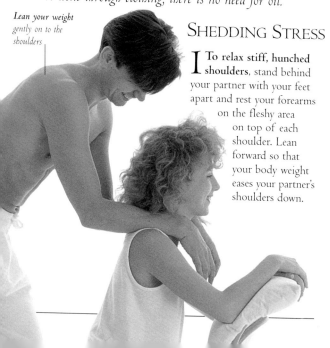

2 **Stroke around the neck** and shoulders. Then, with both hands working together, knead the muscles at the top of one shoulder. Squeeze and release the flesh, pushing it from hand to hand. Work across the shoulder and the top of the arm. Repeat on the other shoulder.

3 **Place your thumbs** below the shoulder blades at either side of the spine and lean on to them. Hold the pressure for a few seconds, then release, glide up a little and repeat. Continue to the top of the spine, then work all over the shoulders.

4 **Make stimulating circular pressures** with your fingers all over the head. Try to move the scalp without pulling the hair. Repeat over the forehead, around the temples and behind the ears. Finish the massage by stroking alternate hands calmly down the back.

PREPARING TO TRAVEL

THE VERSATILITY OF ESSENTIAL OILS makes them valuable in a travel kit. As well as being soothing, they are useful antiseptics and insect repellants. Take ready-made remedies for likely complaints in plastic bottles, and extra essential oils and carrier oil that can be blended during your stay. Label all bottles carefully. For diluting essential oils, see page 21.

TRAVEL KIT ESSENTIALS

Key essential oils: Take **Roman chamomile** oil to soothe, **tea tree** to treat minor cuts and infections, and **lavender** for insect bites, sores and insomnia. Dilute the oils in a carrier oil such as **sweet almond oil**.

Antiseptic blend:
Diluted tea tree and lavender oils can be applied to stings and minor cuts.

Insect repellant room spray

Sweet almond carrier oil

Roman chamomile oil

Tea tree oil

Lavender oil

Antiseptic blend

Insect repellant room spray:
Blend 1 drop each of tea tree, eucalyptus and peppermint, 2 drops each of lemon-grass and geranium, and 100 ml of cooled, boiled water in a spray bottle.

Vapour ring: Place on a light bulb or radiator, with 7–8 drops of essential oil inside. As the oil evaporates, it scents the room.

Bath blend for mild sunburn:
Add diluted chamomile and lavender oils to a bath.

Massage oil for stomach upset:
Use diluted geranium, rosemary and peppermint oils.

Compress blend: Apply a cold compress made with geranium, lavender and chamomile oils to bruises or sprains (see page 93).

Jet lag blends: Diluted orange and geranium oils refresh, while lavender and chamomile have a relaxing effect. Use the blends in a bath or massage, or heat the oils in a vaporizer (see page 91).

Bath blend for
mild sunburn

Massage oil for
stomach upset

Compress blend
and face-cloth

Vapour
ring

Refreshing jet lag blend   Relaxing jet lag blend

IN THE CAR

REVIVING SELF-MASSAGE STROKES help dispel both the drowsiness that can set in during long drives and the frustration of sitting in heavy traffic. Combat irritation and fatigue by taking regular rest breaks during long journeys and practise these simple movements to release muscular tension and increase energy.

EASING TENSE HANDS

Relax strained muscles by supporting one palm with the fingers of your other hand and, with your thumb, stroke from each knuckle in turn down the furrow to the wrist. Repeat on the other hand.

SELF-HELP TIPS

❖ *At the wheel, consciously relax your shoulders and make sure your back is well supported.*

❖ *For car sickness, chew fresh root ginger 30 minutes before driving and at intervals during the journey. Pressing on the middle of the inner wrist 3 finger-widths below the top crease for 10–15 seconds also helps.*

❖ *Place 2–3 drops of lemon or peppermint essential oil on cotton wool to freshen stale air.*

INSTANT INVIGORATION

Work firmly
and methodically
all over your head

Stimulate circulation in your scalp
and alleviate tension headaches by
making firm circular movements with
your fingertips. Work up from your
forehead and all over your head.

DURING DELAYS

FEW OF US ESCAPE the occasional delay in an airport lounge or train station when we are travelling. The frustration caused by waiting for planes, trains, ferries or buses can lead to clenched teeth, a tight jaw and headaches. The following invigorating massage movements help to release bottled-up tension and restore patience.

ENERGIZING EFFECTS

SELF-HELP TIPS

❖ Inhale 2–3 drops of essential oil placed on cotton wool: lavender calms, rosemary uplifts, and rose evokes a summer scene.

❖ Breathe slowly and deeply (see page 26) to calm yourself.

❖ Splash cold water on your face for instant refreshment.

❖ If you are with a friend, massage each other's shoulders (see pages 76–77) to prevent the build-up of tension.

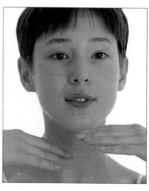

1 To revitalize yourself, pat beneath your chin with the back of your hands. Then use your fingertips to tap lightly and rapidly all over your face.

2 To ease tension in your jaw, roll the skin of each cheek with the back of your fingers, one hand after the other. Work from chin to ear on each side.

AFTER CARRYING LUGGAGE

ALMOST EVERYONE HOLDS SOME TENSION in their neck and shoulders. Carrying heavy bags and suitcases increases the strain on this area, causing stiffness and inflexibility. A soothing self-massage around the neck and shoulders is the perfect antidote to over-exerted muscles and can be performed anywhere, from a hotel room to a bus stop.

REVIVING THE NECK & SHOULDERS

I **To ease aches and pains**, stroke your right shoulder with your left hand. Circle the whole area, applying extra pressure where you feel most tense. Then stroke down your arm to your elbow. Repeat several times, then work on the other side with your right hand.

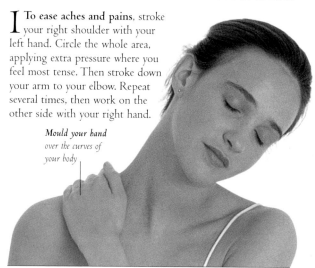

Mould your hand *over the curves of your body*

2 **Soothe tension** by applying circular pressures with your fingers on either side of your spine, starting at the top of the neck and working along the hairline.

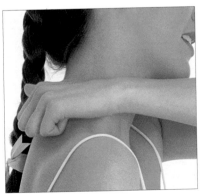

3 **To restore circulation**, loosely clench your left hand into a fist and gently pound your right shoulder. Repeat on the other side with your right hand.

ON THE PLANE

FLYING CAN BE STRESSFUL: anxiety is a common problem, pressure changes affect the ears, and cramped conditions lead to stiffness. Self-massage strokes calm the nerves, ease blocked ears and, by stimulating the circulation, prevent stiff legs and swollen ankles. For comfort, distribute your weight equally in your seat, loosen shoe laces, and wear a neck pillow.

FEELING AT EASE

1 To distribute your weight well, tilt your seat back and place a small pillow behind your middle back. Rest your feet on your hand luggage under the seat in front.

2 ◁ To calm the nerves, close your eyes and stroke your fingers from the bridge of the nose, over the eyebrows to the temples.

RELIEVING BLOCKED EARS

1 **Remove the neck pillow** for ease of movement and apply small circular pressures with the fingers of both hands to the front of your ears, just above your jaw bone. This has a stimulating effect and helps to release pressure in the ears.

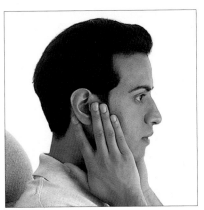

2 **Place your index fingers** behind each ear, keeping the remaining fingers in front. Make slow circular movements with all your fingers in an anticlockwise direction to help improve lymphatic flow and soothe any discomfort.

SOOTHING STROKES

1 △ **With alternate hands**, gently grasp and release the flesh on your thigh. Repeat several times, then stroke one hand after the other up the thigh. Repeat on the other leg.

2 ◁ **Squeeze each side of your calf** with the palms and fingers of alternate hands. Stroke the calf, then repeat on the other leg.

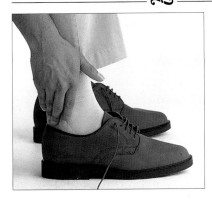

3 **To improve circulation** in the ankles and help ease swelling, circle the fingertips of both hands around the bone on either side of your ankle. You may need to lift your foot to reach. Repeat on the other ankle.

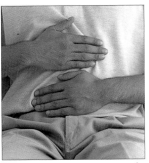

4 **Calm a nervous stomach** by stroking around the navel in a clockwise direction with one hand following the other. Try to keep the stroke as smooth and fluid as possible.

SELF-HELP TIPS

❖ *Drinking fresh carrot juice has been found to prevent oxygen deprivation during flights.*

❖ *To avoid dehydration, drink plenty of non-carbonated mineral water.*

❖ *Release trapped air in the ears by sucking boiled sweets or yawning, especially when the plane takes off and lands.*

❖ *Rotate your feet to counter swelling around the ankles.*

COMBATING JET LAG

AFTER LONG-DISTANCE AIR TRAVEL, the body and mind can suffer from disorientation as the body's internal 24-hour clock struggles to adjust to its new environment. Calming or energizing massage strokes relieve the lethargy or insomnia that often occur and help regulate sleeping patterns. To enhance the effect, use aromatic oils (see page 21).

SLEEP-INDUCING STROKE

SELF-HELP TIPS

❖ Set your watch to the local time, adjust your eating patterns to suit the new environment and try not to sleep during daylight.

❖ Take an energizing walk in the fresh air to replenish vitality.

❖ Soak in a bath with a relaxing or invigorating blend of essential oils (see page 89).

❖ Induce sleep or uplift the mind by burning essential oils in a vaporizer (see page 91).

Encourage sleep by closing your eyes and stroking one hand after the other up your forehead from the bridge of the nose to the hairline. Enjoy the deep sense of relaxation.

WAKE-UP EXERCISE

To revive a tired face, stretch your lips over your teeth to form an "O" shape, and apply circular pressures with the index and middle fingers of each hand around your mouth and chin. Then make exaggerated "aah, ooh, eee, uuu" sounds.

USEFUL OILS

To relax:
chamomile, lavender
To wake up:
geranium, orange

ON THE BEACH

*WHAT COULD BE MORE PAMPERING than a relaxing back
massage while lying on the beach? As you apply sunscreen
to your partner's back, try these soothing strokes. Choose a
shady area and rinse any salt water off your hands
and your partner's back before starting. Work smoothly
and rhythmically for a soporific effect.*

SOOTHING BACK MASSAGE

I Kneel by your partner's side, facing
toward the head, and place your hands
on either side of the spine at the base of
the back. Stroke firmly up the back and
around the shoulders, then glide down
the sides and pull up at the waist.
Repeat several times.

Position your hands to face
toward your partner's head

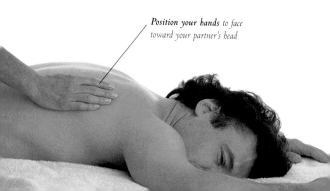

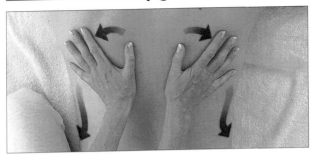

2 **Place your hands together** on the lower back. Stroke up to the ribs, then fan out and glide down the sides. Repeat the stroke, working up the back.

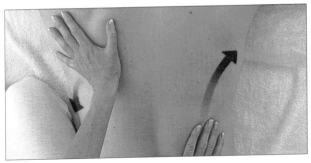

3 **With both hands** at the lower back, stroke one hand up to the shoulder. Glide down the side as your other hand repeats the stroke. Aim for a fluid effect.

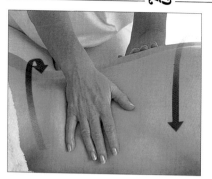

4 **Turn to face across the back.** Place one hand on each side of the waist with your fingers facing away from you. Firmly pull up the sides of the body to squeeze the waist, then lightly glide your hands toward each other.

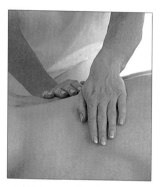

5 **Slide your hands** past each other and down the other side. Repeat, gradually working up the back with this criss-crossing movement. Finish with gentle strokes all over the back.

SELF-HELP TIPS

❖ *For maximum comfort, wear a hat and sunglasses while massaging your partner.*

❖ *To avoid burning, frequently reapply sunscreen to yourself and your partner, especially after swimming. Apply sunscreen thickly and evenly, paying attention to sensitive areas such as the nose and ears.*

❖ *If sitting in the sun, drink plenty of cold water to prevent dehydration and heat exhaustion.*

EASING SYMPTOMS OF STRESS

The massage programmes on the following pages help to combat common stress-related ailments, from headaches and backache to lethargy and insomnia.

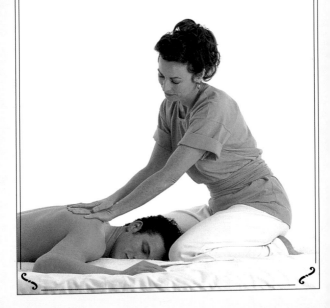

INSOMNIA

MASSAGE IS AN IDEAL REMEDY for insomnia, since hypnotic strokes promote sleep without the side-effects of sleeping pills. Massage someone who has difficulty sleeping for 20 minutes at night, using a 1% dilution (see page 21) of essential oils. Shiatsu self-massage is also effective. It may take a few treatments to break the habit of insomnia, so persevere.

SOPORIFIC STROKES

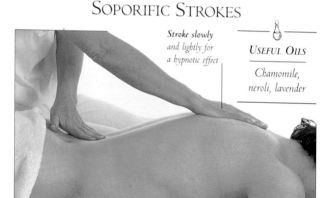

Stroke slowly and lightly for a hypnotic effect

USEFUL OILS

Chamomile, neroli, lavender

I **Kneel by your partner's side** facing toward the head. Slowly and continuously glide one hand after the other down the back, lifting each one at the bottom and returning it to the neck.

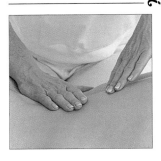

2 **For a warm, comforting sensation**, turn to face the body and place your hands on the lower back with fingertips pointing toward each other. Glide your hands back and forth in a gentle, smooth stroke.

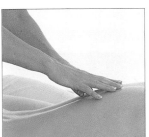

3 **Turn toward the head** again, and with the fingertips of both hands, stroke very lightly down the back, returning to the neck when you reach the small of the back. This "feather touch" should be as gentle and fluid as possible.

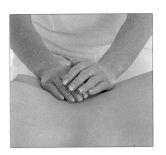

4 **Place slightly cupped hands** over the small of the back. Hold them there for a few minutes and gently flatten your hands to release the gathered heat into your partner's body. Then lift your hands away very slowly and imperceptibly.

Shiatsu Self-help for Insomnia

I **Sit comfortably** with one knee bent and your other leg straight. Rest one elbow on your knee and apply pressure with your thumb to the bridge of your nose, leaning your body weight on to your thumb. Hold the pressure for 10–15 seconds.

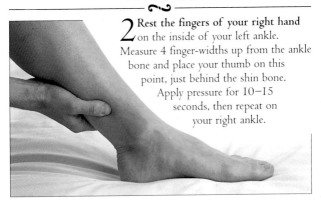

2 Rest the fingers of your right hand on the inside of your left ankle. Measure 4 finger-widths up from the ankle bone and place your thumb on this point, just behind the shin bone. Apply pressure for 10–15 seconds, then repeat on your right ankle.

3 With your right thumb, press the depression on the side of your left wrist, below the little finger. Hold for 10–15 seconds, then repeat on your right wrist.

SELF-HELP TIPS

❖ *Soak in a restorative bath containing ylang ylang, lavender or chamomile oil (see page 88).*

❖ *Place a drop of diluted lavender oil on your pillow (see page 21).*

❖ *Drink calming chamomile tea.*

❖ *Breathe deeply: lie with your hands placed on your abdomen. Inhale through your nose, feeling your abdomen expand; exhale, letting the abdomen sink down.*

LETHARGY

BRISK, SELF-MASSAGE MOVEMENTS can provide instant energy if you are feeling tired and lethargic. Massage stimulates the circulation, bringing fresh oxygenated blood to the area and dispelling fatigue. Be as gentle or as energetic as you like with the following massage strokes. They should leave you feeling refreshed and regenerated, not black and blue!

ENERGY BOOSTS

1 ◁ **To wake yourself up**, rhythmically tap the fingertips of both hands over your whole face in an energetic and galloping motion.

2 **Gently pound** all over your head with loosely clenched fists to stimulate the circulation. Then, with open, relaxed hands, lightly slap your head.

3 With the fingers and thumb of your right hand, lightly pluck the flesh at the top of your left arm. Keep your wrists floppy to avoid hurting yourself and work down to the wrist. Then repeat on your right arm.

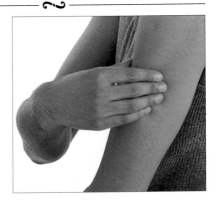

SELF-HELP TIPS

❖ *To help banish fatigue, apply pressure for 5–10 seconds to the shiatsu point on the centre of the sole of the foot, just below the ball of the foot.*

❖ *Take a reviving bath with diluted jasmine or rose essential oil (see page 88).*

❖ *Shake your hands and feet, and swing your arms around to increase blood circulation and wake yourself up.*

4 Raise your left leg slightly and pummel your thigh and buttock with loose fists, keeping your wrists flexible and the movement vigorous. Work down the length of your leg, then repeat on your right thigh.

HANGOVERS

MASSAGE WITH AROMATIC OILS can relieve the headaches, muscular fatigue and listlessness that afflict hangover sufferers. The first signs of tension are visible in the face — a constricted forehead and tight jaw — so focus on these areas. Use a weak blend of oils (see page 21).

RAPID RELIEF

1 **To induce a feeling of calmness**, sit behind your partner's head and cup both hands over the forehead. Gently press down for a minute, then gradually release the pressure.

Place one palm on top of the other

USEFUL OILS

Lavender, peppermint, rosemary

2 **Clear blocked sinuses** by applying pressure with the middle finger of each hand to the shiatsu points under the cheekbones, in line with the mid-point of each eye. Then, to ease headaches, press firmly on the temples.

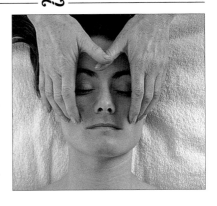

3 **Sandwich the jaw** between your hands with your fingers and thumbs facing each other. Then stroke alternate hands up from the chin to the temples. Repeat 6 times.

SELF-HELP TIPS

❖ Press on the crown of the head for a few seconds to alleviate lethargy and headaches.

❖ Use lavender or peppermint oil in a cold compress (see page 93) for the forehead.

❖ Inhale a drop of peppermint oil placed on cotton wool to relieve nausea.

❖ Drink cold water to counter dehydration and chamomile tea to soothe and calm.

HEADACHES

THERE ARE MANY CAUSES of headaches, but all result in taut muscles in the forehead and neck and restricted blood flow. Massaging a partner around these areas lifts tension and stimulates circulation. Use diluted oils (see page 21) and vary the strokes from gentle gliding to deep pressures. Self-massage on shiatsu points also provides relief.

RELAXING THE NECK

I **Kneel behind your partner's head,** placing your hands behind the shoulders. Stroke up the neck, then glide your hands down the sides of the neck to the collar bones, and around the shoulders.

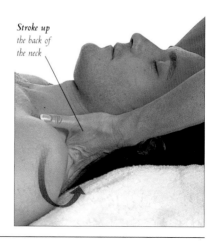

Stroke up the back of the neck

USEFUL OILS

Tension headaches: chamomile, lavender

Digestive headaches: rosemary, peppermint

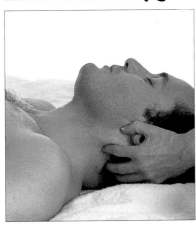

2 To stimulate blood flow and release tight muscles, carefully apply firm circular pressures with the fingers of both hands all around the base of the skull.

3 Stroke one hand after the other up one side of the neck from the shoulder to the base of the skull, leaning slightly toward the side you are working on. Keep the strokes smooth and fluid. Repeat on the other side of the neck.

FACE MASSAGE

1 ▷ **To relieve tension in the head**, place your thumbs on the bridge of the nose and stroke them out to the temples. Repeat, working up the forehead to the hairline.

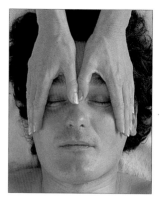

2 **Stroke your thumbs** from the forehead down the bridge of the nose, under the cheekbones and up to the temples. Apply a deep pressure here. Repeat several times.

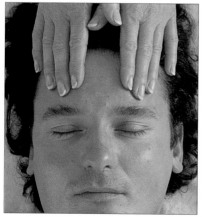

3 ◁ **Apply circular pressures** with your fingers all over the forehead, from the centre out toward the temples. Work slowly and rhythmically: upward circles tend to be invigorating while downward ones are more calming.

4 **Squeeze the eyebrows** between your thumbs and index fingers, working from the bridge of the nose to the temples. Press the temples gently, then repeat the whole movement 3 times.

5 **To ease a taut scalp**, grasp a handful of hair at the roots and gently pull it toward you. Then glide your fingers through the hair and repeat the stroke, alternating hands.

SELF-HELP TIPS

❖ *For rapid headache relief, apply a cold compress to your forehead and over your eyes (see page 93).*

❖ *Rub diluted lavender or peppermint oil (see page 21) into your temples.*

❖ *To ease constricted muscles and improve circulation, submerge your wrists in hot water.*

SHIATSU SELF-HELP FOR HEADACHES

1 **To ease pain**, fold a small, damp towel into a strip, wrap it around your forehead, and tie it at the base of the skull. Pull the ends to exert gentle pressure.

2 **Press your thumbs** into the indentations at the base of the skull, on either side of the spine. Hold for 5–10 seconds, resting your fingers on the head.

3 **Use the thumb of one hand** to press the depression formed by the two tendons at the base of the other thumb. Press for 5–10 seconds, supporting the wrist with your fingers, then repeat on your other hand.

Apply firm pressure to your temples to squeeze away tension

4 Apply pressure with your thumbs to your temples. Breathe deeply, imagining you are squeezing tension from your head. Then rotate your thumbs.

BACKACHE

WHEN NOT A RESULT of muscular strain, backache can be a physical manifestation of mental stress. Soothe a partner by giving a massage with diluted oils (see page 21) or try self-massage through your clothes. Slow, rhythmic movements calm and deep pressures ease tautness. Check the cautions on page 24 before starting.

SOOTHING SENSATIONS

1 **Kneel behind your partner's head** and rest your hands at the top of the back on either side of the spine. Stroke down the back and fan out over the hips. Glide up the sides and repeat about 6 times.

——— § ———

USEFUL OILS

Frankincense, marjoram, orange

Stroke your hands *as far as you can reach down the back*

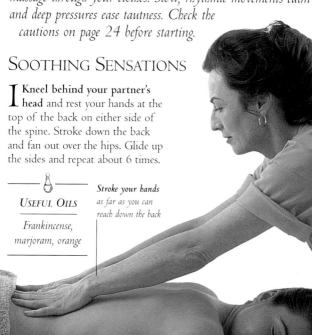

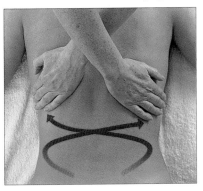

2 **Stroke down the back** as in step 1. Fan out at the hips, then pull up at the sides and glide your hands across the spine, criss-crossing the body. Work up to the shoulders, forming figures of eight. Repeat 3 times.

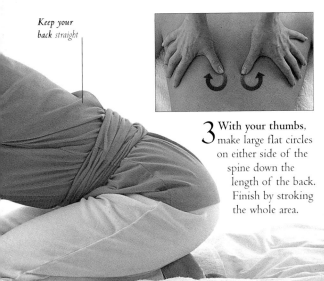

Keep your back straight

3 With your thumbs, make large flat circles on either side of the spine down the length of the back. Finish by stroking the whole area.

SELF-TREATMENT FOR BACKACHE

I **To relax your back**, sit comfortably and place your hands, with fingers pointing downward, on your lower back at either side of the spine. Stroke firmly down the back, fanning your hands over your hips, and glide back. Repeat 6 times.

Ease away tension in your lower back with deep circular movements

2 Place your thumbs on the middle of your back at either side of the spine, with fingers resting on your hips. Apply pressure with your thumbs, then release and repeat a little further up the back. Continue as far as you can reach.

3 Lie on your left side with your right knee bent over your left leg. Using the fingers of your right hand, apply circular pressures around the sacrum. Then stroke the whole area.

STIFF NECK & SHOULDERS

MOST OF US SUFFER from occasional neck and shoulder pain. Bad posture, anxiety, draughts, even the heaviness of our heads can lead to tense neck and shoulder muscles. Massage helps by easing contracted muscles and bringing new blood to the area. Seat your partner astride a chair leaning on to a cushion. See pages 38–39 for extra techniques.

RELEASING TENSION

I **Relax the area** by placing your hands at the base of the neck. Stroke them firmly out across the top of the shoulders and back to the neck, sweeping up to the base of the skull. Repeat about 6 times.

Keep your hands open and relaxed

2 **Stroke your right hand** in a clockwise circle over the top of one shoulder and around the shoulder blade. Let the left hand follow, lifting it over the right when they meet to form a fluid stroke. Repeat on the opposite shoulder.

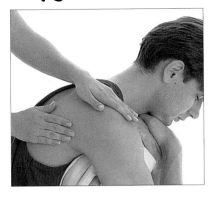

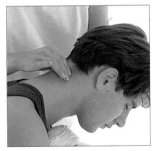

3 **Support the head** with your left hand. With your right, stroke up the neck, then, with your fingers, apply circular pressures to the neck and base of the skull. Finish by smoothly stroking the neck and shoulders.

SELF-HELP TIPS

❖ *To relax your shoulders, raise them to your ears. Hold for a few seconds then release.*

❖ *Gently stretch your neck and alleviate tension by placing your right hand on your left shoulder and tilting your head to the right. Hold for several seconds, then repeat on the other side.*

❖ *Avoid carrying heavy bags that place excessive strain on your neck and shoulders.*

STOMACH ACHES

STOMACH ACHES, whether caused by indigestion, tension or menstrual pains, can be soothed with massage. Some people are apprehensive about having their abdomens touched, so keep your strokes smooth and gentle, using a teaspoon of diluted essential oils (see page 21). To help relax the stomach and back muscles, place a pillow under your partner's knees.

SENSITIVE TOUCHES

USEFUL OILS

Chamomile, orange, clary sage, peppermint

I **Kneel by your partner's right side** facing the abdomen. Rest your left hand on the lower ribs and, with your right hand, circle around the navel in a clockwise direction. Gradually increase the pressure, building up a confident and steady rhythm.

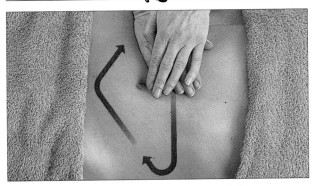

2 **To melt away tension**, rest your left hand on your right hand and apply slight pressure. Release, then repeat, working in a triangle around the navel.

3 **With flat, open hands**, lightly knead each side of the abdomen in turn. Gently grasp some flesh with one hand and ease it into the other. Finish by stroking the abdomen.

SELF-HELP TIPS

❖ *For period pain, squeeze the ankle on either side of the Achilles tendon for 10 seconds.*

❖ *To relieve indigestion, measure 3 finger-widths below the knee and press behind the shin bone for 5–10 seconds.*

❖ *Drink peppermint tea after a meal to help digestion.*

SPORTS ACHES & PAINS

MASSAGE, EITHER WITH A PARTNER or self-massage, is the perfect adjunct to exercise. It improves recovery rate, and by hastening the elimination of metabolic wastes, eases stiffness and cramps. Ask your partner to lie face down. Diluted essential oils can be applied in step 2 (see page 21).

EASING TIGHTNESS

I **Sit facing your partner's side**, resting your hands on the back at a comfortable distance apart. Push the flesh away with the heels of your hands, then lightly pull your fingers back to create a rocking motion.

Keep the movement relaxed and rhythmic

USEFUL OILS

Marjoram, rosemary, eucalyptus

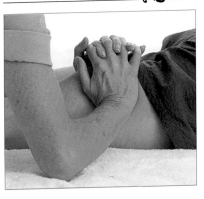

2 **Kneel by your partner's legs.** Interlace your fingers and rest the heels of your hands on either side of one thigh. Apply compression to the large muscle groups by squeezing and releasing the flesh, working down the length of the leg.

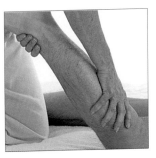

3 **Raise the calf** and support the ankle with one hand. Stroke your other hand down to the knee, then glide back, change hands and repeat the stroke. Try to keep the movement continuous.

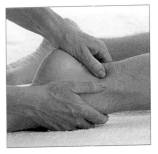

4 **Lower the leg**, sliding one hand under the foot. With the thumb and fingers of your other hand, squeeze and release the flesh around the Achilles tendon. Then repeat steps 2–4 on the other leg.

SELF-MASSAGE FOR STRAINED MUSCLES

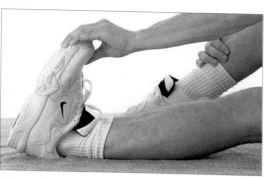

1 **For calf cramp**, sit with your affected leg straight and the other knee bent. Pull the toes of your straight leg toward you, feeling the calf muscle stretch. Hold until the pain eases.

2 **For hamstring cramp**, lie on your back and raise your affected leg, keeping the other bent. Firmly stroke the back of your thigh with alternate hands.

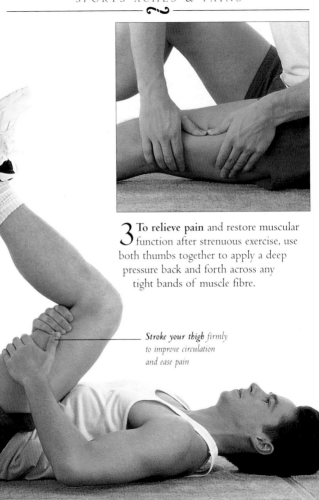

3 **To relieve pain** and restore muscular
function after strenuous exercise, use
both thumbs together to apply a deep
pressure back and forth across any
tight bands of muscle fibre.

*Stroke your thigh firmly
to improve circulation
and ease pain*

TIRED HANDS & FEET

WE USE OUR HANDS AND FEET constantly, so it is not surprising that they often feel tired and stiff. Both contain a rich supply of nerve endings, and massaging them benefits the whole body. Hands and feet are easy to reach and as there is no need to undress, they are ideal areas to initiate someone into the joys of massage. Start with the hands, then the feet.

RELAXING THE HANDS

1 Dissolve tension in the hand by sandwiching it between your palms. Then stroke firmly from the knuckles to the wrist.

2 Turn the hand over and support it with your fingers. Hook your little fingers over your partner's thumb and little finger and gently open the palm to stretch it. Then firmly fan your thumbs out across the palm and, with one thumb, make deep circular pressures all over the palm.

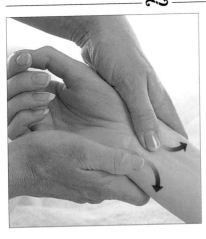

3 Slide your hands up to support the wrist. Fan both thumbs firmly up the inner wrist and out to the sides, then glide down. Continue with one thumb after the other. Then turn the wrist over and repeat the stroke.

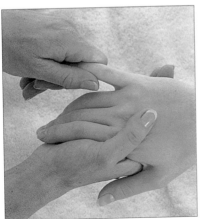

4 Hold the palm face down in one hand. With your other hand, squeeze along the length of each finger in turn and make circular pressures around the joints. Finish by gently pulling each finger. Follow the whole massage sequence on the other hand.

REVIVING THE FEET

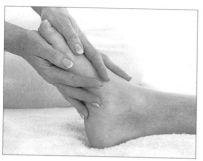

1 **Kneel by your partner's feet.** Sandwich your palms around one foot with your fingers facing away from you. Then stroke firmly and rhythmically toward the ankle, gliding back to repeat.

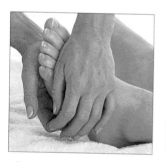

2 **Place one palm** across the top of the foot, the other underneath, just below the toes. Apply pressure and make circular movements with both hands to loosen the muscles in the toes and invigorate the area.

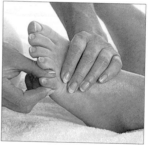

3 **Hold the foot** between the thumb and fingers of one hand. Use the thumb and index finger of your other hand to squeeze and rotate each toe in turn. Stroke the foot and repeat each step on the other foot.

USING AROMATIC PREPARATIONS

Fragrant oils can be used in baths and steam treatments, scented sprays and room vaporizers to soothe the body and mind, and enhance well-being.

RESTORATIVE BATHS

THERE IS NO BETTER PLACE to relax and shed the stress of the day than in a bath of warm, fragrant water. Diluted essential oils, added to a bath either singly or as a mixture, can soothe jangled nerves, relieve muscular aches and pains, stimulate or sedate. Bathing by candle-light enhances the effect, transporting you to a haven of tranquillity.

PREPARING FOR THE BATH

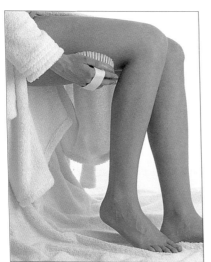

1 **Dilute 5 drops** of your chosen essential oil in 10 ml of carrier oil (see page 21), or try the blends opposite. For a shower, add 12 drops of essential oil to 30 ml of liquid soap.

2 ◁ **Before you step into the bath** or shower, stimulate the skin by brushing your whole body with a natural fibre skin brush, using brisk, circular strokes.

AROMATIC BATH BLENDS

TO ENJOY THE FULL EFFECTS of the essential oils in the bath, avoid very hot water and disperse the blend well.

RELAXING BLEND

Essential oils
2 drops each of neroli and sandalwood
1 drop clary sage
Carrier oil
10 ml sweet almond

FOR ACHING LIMBS

Essential oils
2 drops each of lavender and rosemary
1 drop marjoram
Carrier oil
10 ml sweet almond

Follow the blending method on page 21.

INVIGORATING BLEND

Essential oils
2 drops each of rosemary and juniper
1 drop geranium
Carrier oil
10 ml sweet almond

MILK AND HONEY BATH

Essential oil
10-25 drops geranium
Base
1 tsp liquid detergent
110 ml sweet almond oil
25 ml vodka
55 ml milk
1 tsp honey
1 egg

Mix ingredients in a blender on low speed. This recipe makes enough for 8 baths.

Follow the blending method on page 21.

ROOM FRESHENERS

TO PROMOTE A PEACEFUL atmosphere in your home, workplace or hotel room, scent the air with essential oils. Room sprays are simple to make and have instant impact. Vaporizers consist of a small bowl containing essential oil and water. A candle is lit below the bowl and the oils release their aroma.

SCENTED SPRAYS

CREATE A FRESH and fragrant environment by adding 2 drops of essential oil to 100 ml of cooled, boiled water in a plant sprayer. Shake well and spray around the room.

REFRESHING BLEND	LUXURIOUS BLEND
❖	❖
Essential oils	**Essential oils**
1 drop each of lemon-grass and lavender	*1 drop each of orange and frankincense*
Base	**Base**
100 ml cooled, boiled water	*100 ml cooled, boiled water*

Add ingredients to a plant sprayer.

VAPORIZERS

FILL THE BOWL of the vaporizer with water and 2–4 drops of essential oil. Light a small candle and place it below the bowl.

UPLIFTING BLEND

Essential oils
1 drop each of orange, juniper
and frankincense

Base
water

SLEEP-INDUCING BLEND

Essential oils
1 drop each of Roman chamomile,
neroli and lavender

Base
water

Add ingredients to the bowl of the vaporizer.

Bowl

CAUTION: Do not let the water evaporate completely, as the bowl may crack. Keep away from children.

Place small candle here

STEAMS & COMPRESSES

Facial steams, or inhalations, are used for alleviating respiratory problems, congested sinuses, sore throats and coughs, as well as deep cleaning the skin. Do not use inhalations if you suffer from asthma. Warm compresses help relieve backache and abdominal pains; cold compresses ease headaches, swollen joints, bruises, sprains and cramps.

MAKING A FACIAL STEAM

Fill a large bowl with boiling water and add 2-6 drops of essential oil. Lean over the bowl, covering your head with a towel to trap the steam. Close your eyes and breathe deeply for five minutes. For skin problems, use no more than once a week.

FOR COLDS & COUGHS

❖

Essential oils
2 drops each of tea tree, sandalwood and eucalyptus
Base
boiling water

FOR MENTAL FATIGUE

❖

Essential oils
2 drops each of clary sage, rosemary and geranium
Base
boiling water

Add ingredients to a large bowl.

MAKING A COMPRESS

USE HOT WATER FOR a warm compress and cold water for a cold one. Follow the steps below, and apply the compress for ten to twenty minutes, re-soaking the cloth as necessary.

1 Add up to 6 drops of blended oil (see page 21) to a bowl of water.

2 Stir, then place a face-cloth on the surface to collect the oil. Wring out, then apply to the affected area.

FOR TENSION HEADACHES

❖

Essential oils
2 drops each of chamomile and lavender
Carrier oil
10 ml sunflower

FOR SPRAINS & CRAMPS

❖

Essential oils
2 drops each of juniper and chamomile
1 drop eucalyptus
Carrier oil
10 ml sunflower

Follow the blending method on page 21.

INDEX

Page numbers in **bold**
indicate main oil entries.

ACKNOWLEDGMENTS

For mail order supply of oils and
details of massage courses, send a
stamped self-addressed envelope to:

Clare Maxwell-Hudson
P.O. Box 457
London NW2 4BR

AUTHOR'S ACKNOWLEDGMENTS
I would like to thank my colleagues,
clients and students for their
encouragement, and especially Gill
Whitworth and Amina Shah;
Rhiannon Lewis for research on
essential oils; everyone at Dorling
Kindersley, especially Nell, Helen,
Susannah, Toni and Daphne; Sandra
Lousada for her beautiful photos.

DORLING KINDERSLEY would like to
thank Ron at Clark Davis & Co. Ltd;
New World Aurora; Abdul Ahmed,
Hanna Andrews at Models I,
Rachana Devidayal, Vera Fortes,
Martha Fraton, David Gillingwater,
Frances Graham, Dorte Jensen, Paul
Johnson, Barbara Jones, Sarah King,
Eve Tomlinson, Charlie P. at Models
I Men, Paul Surety and Karen Su
Ying Woo for modelling; Ellen
Kramer at Artistic Licence for make-
up; Michele Walker for help with art
direction; Karen Ruane for DTP;
Kate Chapman for the index.

PICTURE CREDITS
Key: t = top c = centre b = bottom
Photography by Sandra Lousada
except: Tim Ridley 8t,c, 9, 10, 11t,
12t, 13t, 14t, 15t, 16t, 17, 18t, 20,
21, 40, 41, 87, 90, 91, 93; Steve
Gorton 4, 7, 8b, 12b, 13b, 14b, 15b,
16b, 18b; Dave King 11b.
Illustrations: Karen Cochrane for
arrows; Charlotte Wess for plants.